W9-ANM-505

MURALS

FRANKLIN PIERCE
COLLEGE LIBRARY
RINDGE, N.H. 03461

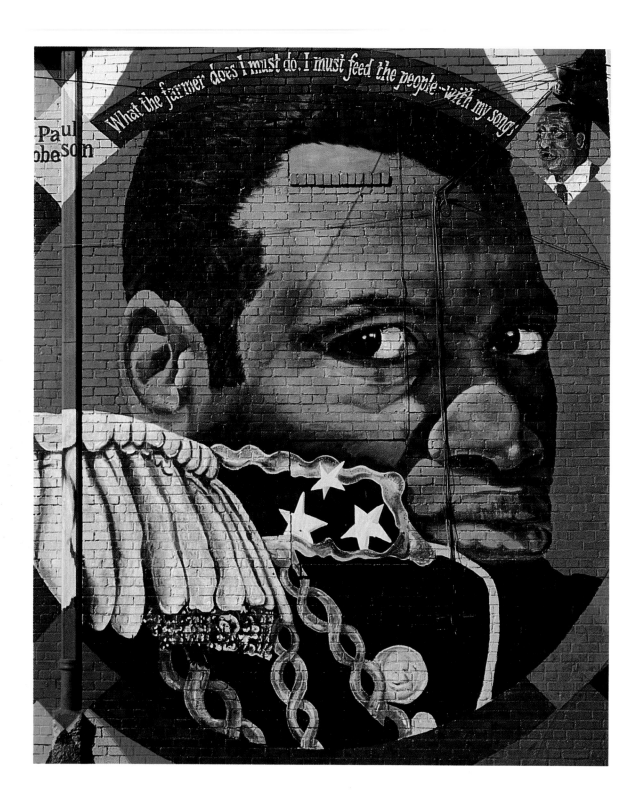

MURALS

CAVE,
CATHEDRAL,
TO STREET

Michael Capek

L LERNER PUBLICATIONS COMPANY • MINNEAPOLIS

On the front cover: (top) Cave painting at Lascaux, France (photo by French Government Tourist Office); (middle) Michelangelo, *The Creation of Adam* (detail), Sistine Chapel, Rome, Italy (THE BETTMANN ARCHIVE); (bottom) Judith Baca and community members, *The Great Wall of Los Angeles* (detail), Studio City, California (© Nancy Hoyt Belcher). On the back cover: Diego Rivera, *Dream of a Sunday in the Alameda* (detail), Hotel del Prado, Mexico City, Mexico (Art Resource, New York/reproduction authorized by the National Institute of Fine Arts and Literature, Mexico).

Page one: Herman Krumpholtz/Juleen Designs, Inc., Butler Square Mural, Minneapolis, Minnesota. Page two: detail from a mural at the Seven Stages Theater in Atlanta, Georgia.

METRIC CONVERSION FACTORS

When you know	Multiply by	To find
feet	.30	meters
inches	2.54	centimeters
meters	3.3	feet
miles	1.6	kilometers
pounds	0.45	kilograms
Celcius	1.8, add 32	Fahrenheit
Fahrenheit	subtract 32, multiply by 0.555	Celcius

Copyright © 1996 by Lerner Publications Company
All rights reserved. International copyright secured. No part of this book may be reproduced or transmitted in any form or by any means, electronic or mechanical, including photocopying and recording, or by any information storage or retrieval system, without permission in writing from Lerner Publications Company, except for the inclusion of brief quotations in an acknowledged review.

LIBRARY OF CONGRESS CATALOGING-IN-PUBLICATION DATA
Capek, Michael.
    Murals: cave, cathedral, to street / Michael Capek.
      p. cm.
    Includes index.
    Summary: Describes murals of various times and cultures including those in the United States Capitol, murals of Diego Rivera and of the Italian Renaissance, and Egyptian tomb paintings.
    ISBN 0-8225-2065-6 (alk. paper)
    1. Mural painting and decoration—Juvenile literature. [1. Mural painting and decoration.] I. Title.
ND2550.C36 1995
751.7'3—dc20   95-346

Manufactured in the United States of America
1 2 3 4 5 6 – JR – 01 00 99 98 97 96

CURR
ND
2550
.C36
1996

CONTENTS

Maps

INTRODUCTION

Not all of the world's greatest paintings hang in museums. Some decorate the interiors of churches, temples, and public buildings. Many are outdoors, enlivening walls or the sides of buildings. These gigantic pictures painted on walls or ceilings are called murals.

Murals are large paintings done directly on the surface of a wall, ceiling, or, occasionally, on the floor. If the surface is in rough condition, the artist might have to do some preparatory work first, such as removing loose particles and dirt with a wire brush. Next, he or she might apply plaster or grout to fill in cracks or to make the wall smoother. Finally, the artist might paint the wall white or another light color, so the mural's colors will show up well. Some artists paint their murals on huge sheets of canvas or on wood panels, which are then attached to a wall.

Other artists work in fresco. Fresco is a technique in which paint is applied directly onto wet plaster. The paint mixes with the plaster. When it dries, the paint actually becomes part of the wall. Artists have used this technique for hundreds of years. Although the technique is very difficult, frescoes are beautiful and durable.

A muralist may use several kinds of paint, including oil, watercolor, acrylic, and vinyl. One type of paint that has

Diego Rivera, *The Great City of Tenochtitlán* (detail), National Palace of Fine Arts, Mexico City, Mexico, 1945.

been used for centuries is tempera, a mixture of natural color pigments, water, and egg yolk. Each kind of paint has its own special advantages, and an artist has to decide which one will work best, depending on the location of the mural. The wrong decision about paint may mean the mural won't last longer than the first rain!

Many artists like to apply paint the old-fashioned way, with a brush. Others, however, use anything from a roller to an airbrush, which is a kind of super spray gun. Still others spread the paint on thick with trowels or putty

Three photographs taken over a period of time show how muralist Richard Haas transformed a drab wall of the Kroger Co. in Cincinnati into what appears to be a beautiful, grand building.

An artist paints a mural on canvas, part of a series of murals for CITIBANK in New York.

knives. A few artists even use regular spray cans.

Another mural technique is not a method of painting at all—it's mosaic. Mosaics are created by placing small pieces of stone, glass, metal, or other material (these pieces are called *tesserae*) into a wet mastic, usually plaster or cement. When the mastic dries, the tesserae are held fast and form part of the wall or floor. Skilled artists can arrange the tesserae into all sorts of shapes and patterns. They might let some of the pieces stick out a little, giving the finished mosaic a three-dimensional look.

Whatever technique they use, people do love to paint on walls. It's fun! And murals are an eye-catching way to convey a message.

Interior designers and city planners often use murals to hide an ugly wall or brighten up a shabby street. A good example is the spectacular Heaven Room murals at Burghley House in Lincolnshire, England. Painted by Antonio Verrio in the late 1600s, the murals give guests the illusion of mingling with the gods on Mount Olympus. The figures seem to step right out of the painting into the room.

With the multicolored ceramic mural he created in 1950–51 for Harvard University, Joan Miró transformed a bland, colorless wall of the Graduate Center into a work of art. Miró said he wished "through painting to get closer to the masses of humanity." He does just that every time someone sees and enjoys his mural.

Probably the most vigorous and active muralists today are working in neighborhoods all over the world, covering the walls of old buildings with paintings that carry a message. Many of these murals reveal people's pride in their heritage. The whole community may get involved, and people of different cultures and races come together to create something meaningful and beautiful.

Sometimes people use murals to express their opinions—their political, social, or religious views. Murals can become a sort of artistic shouting match between opposing parties as

each side tries to outdo the other with bigger, brighter, and more provocative murals. Murals often take the form of huge advertisements, pushing an idea, an organization, or a product. Murals in cities might educate people about their culture and heritage. Some of the most famous murals have been done in the spirit of devotion and worship, like those of Michelangelo in the Sistine Chapel in Rome, Italy.

Other murals commemorate important events or people. Since murals can be so large—anywhere from a few feet across to the size of a city block—they can depict complex subjects. Some murals, such as those in the United States Capitol in Washington, D.C., are like gigantic history books, dramatically presenting key events in the life of a city, state, or nation.

But murals are not always so serious. Many of the greatest murals are simply beautiful to look at. Some murals are created solely for decoration—to liven up a dull room, for instance. There are even building-size practical jokes or optical illusions meant to give city dwellers a chuckle or make them shake

their heads in astonishment. One of these was *Hippie Knowhow*, a mural painted in 1971 on a building in Paris, France. (Unfortunately, the mural no longer exists.) It showed two mural painters helplessly hanging from a rope after their scaffold collapsed.

Finally, there is always the anonymous person with a spray can or paintbrush who splashes walls with graffiti, just to show off or to vandalize public places. Although defacing public property is illegal in most places, these creations can be considered a kind of art, too.

Murals, more than most other forms of artistic expression, show us how art has developed over the centuries. To study murals is to study the whole range of art history. Looking at them, we can take a journey backward through time and find records of the people, events, ideas, and artistic styles of specific periods of history.

And what about the motives for creating murals? Have they really changed much since ancient people tried to capture their world in charcoal and red pigment on the walls of caves?

Michelangelo, ceiling of the Sistine Chapel (detail), Vatican Palace, Vatican State, 1508–12.

CONTEMPORARY COMMUNITY MURALS

M any of the most interesting wall paintings being done right now are street or community murals. Some of these are the work of skilled artists who are commissioned to give bare city walls a bright face-lift. Often, though, adults and children from the neighborhood get together to create murals under the direction of a local artist. These murals express people's political concerns or their cultural identities.

In the 1960s, the spirit of confrontation and anger swept across the United States as many people protested the war in Vietnam. Many people also became active in the civil rights movement. Neighborhood groups found a way to express themselves in murals.

One of the earliest community murals was the *Wall of Respect*. In 1967 a group of black artists gathered informally in the South Side of Chicago to paint the side of a semiabandoned building that was scheduled for destruction. The mural showed a number of African American political, historical, and popular figures. The mural disappeared long ago. But the energy that created it has lived on to produce hundreds of community murals in neighborhoods across America.

Community members painted this mural called *In Their Hands* on the entrance to the Hawthorne School in San Francisco.

During the 1960s and 1970s, African Americans, Asian Americans, Native Americans, Latin Americans, women, and other groups expressed their sense of dignity and anger through mural projects. For example, in 1974 artist Alan Okada directed local young people in painting a seven-story mural called *Chi Lai—Arriba—Rise Up!* in New York's Chinatown district. The painting, which faces a school yard, depicts Asian Americans' struggle against racism, poverty, and oppression.

Japanese, Chinese, and other immigrants from the Far East have faced a variety of obstacles, as have other immigrants to the United States. Often, Asian Americans and other minority groups encountered hatred and prejudice. The cities they thought held the promise of a better life turned out to be horrible traps. Most immigrants hoped their children would find the freedom and opportunities they had been denied.

In the mean streets of New York, immigrants often felt as if some predatory creature wanted to squeeze the life out of them. In Okada's mural, an octopus draped in an American flag reaches its tentacles from one side of a splitting tenement building. On the other side, fat, prosperous-looking men are straining to hold the building together. At the top, though, young people of all races break free and raise their arms in triumph. This is Okada's way of saying that children often hold the key to the future. He is also suggesting that strong, energetic people will find a way

to free themselves from the conditions that threaten to hold them back.

Another example of community art with a message is *Winds of Change*, a sweeping street mural in Berkeley, California, by O'Brian Thiele, Osha Neumann, and Daniel Galvez. The huge painting, funded partly by neighborhood merchants, shows a procession of people led by a small boy who blasts a horn at a strange conglomeration of figures: men in suits whose heads are made of TVs, a giant hamburger, and a computer spouting meaningless printouts. A graceful arc of birds joins the people.

It's probably significant that the mural is painted on a building owned by a credit union. (A credit union is a financial organization owned by its members.) The mural suggests that alert, hardworking people can overpower the "suits" who falsely advertise, deceive, or promote waste.

Beautiful murals inspired by an artist's cultural heritage decorate the Daybreak Star Arts Center in Seattle, Washington. Overlooking Puget Sound, the center is a cultural headquarters for American Indians from the Pacific Northwest area. The center exhibits work by artists of many different tribes. Robert Montoya's mural *Deer Hunter* shows a hunter from the San Juan Pueblo in New Mexico. The hunter, dressed in ceremonial costume, chases deer that also appear to be wearing sacred eagle feathers. The painting conveys a deep respect for nature.

José Rey Toledo, mural for the Indian Pueblo Cultural Center, Albuquerque, New Mexico, c. 1977–78.

Another muralist with a conscience is Wyland, whose immense paintings of whales can be seen in the United States, Canada, and Japan. He sometimes chooses not to accept money for his murals, because he hopes people who see them will be motivated to protect these endangered creatures. In the paintings—some of which cover half an acre of wall space—life-size whales dive, leap, and play.

To make sure his whales are authentic, Wyland skin-dives to see them up close. For one painting of a killer whale, Wyland invited marine biologists onto the scaffold where he was working to help him draw the details so they would be accurate.

During a 1993 visit to a marine park in Mexico City, Wyland met Keiko, the whale star of the movie *Free Willy.* "We made eye contact and bonded. It was very emotional," Wyland said. He was told that Keiko was ill from being confined to a small tank. Immediately Wyland offered to paint a mural to decorate the park if the owners would move Keiko to a larger tank. Even though Keiko's keepers already had plans to do that, Wyland asked them to sign an agreement saying they would help the whale before he would go ahead with the mural. Since Wyland could charge as much as $100,000 for one of his whale murals, park officials were more than happy to oblige.

Wyland, *Gray Whale Migration,* Redondo Beach, California, 1991.

Life-size animals also perform on a wall at the Ringling Bros., Barnum & Bailey Circus headquarters in Warrenton, Virginia. Leaping tigers, crazy clowns, majestic elephants, swinging acrobats, and prancing horses fill the 22-by-42-foot mural by William Woodward. Like Wyland with his whales, Woodward studied circus performers and animals at close range for the two years it took him to complete the work.

To paint the acrylic and oil mural, Woodward worked in a warehouse and hung a canvas across a wall. The canvas was so tall, though, that he could only work on half of it at a time. After the top half was painted, Woodward hauled it up and across the ceiling, then began to work on the bottom half. The elephants were especially difficult to do, Woodward said. "There were so many wrinkles that after a while I felt as if I were painting giant raisins," he said.

If there were a "mural capital of the

William Woodward, mural for Ringling Bros., Warrenton, Virginia, 1990.

world," it would have to be Los Angeles, California. Since the establishment of the Citywide Mural Project in 1974, hundreds of "official" murals have been painted on walls throughout the city, not to mention many more spontaneous, "unofficial" ones. Most of the murals are still bright and unmarred after years of exposure to the elements. L.A.'s mild and sunny climate helps, of course. So does the fact that the people in the neighborhoods who helped create the murals feel a sense of ownership and pride in their work and try hard to take care of the murals.

The summer Olympic Games held in Los Angeles in 1984 also sparked the creation of dozens of murals. The Olympics was seen as an opportunity to show the world what muralists in Los Angeles could do. Murals continue to be painted all over the city.

Two Los Angeles murals—*Eyes* and *Mary: 7th Street Altarpiece*—are realistic paintings with a sense of humor. Created by Kent Twitchell and Ruben Brucelyn, the murals show giant faces peering out from inside freeway underpasses. The wall paintings must give motorists caught in traffic the feeling that they're being watched.

Similarly, drivers might look twice at *Freeway Kids* by Glenna Boltuch Avila. Painted on a wall alongside a busy freeway, the mural shows gigantic children skipping, hopping, running, and jumping. It was meant to capture the happy, playful spirit of the 1984 Olympic Games.

Glenna Boltuch Avila, *Freeway Kids,* Highway 101 between Main Street and Los Angeles Street, Los Angeles, 1984.

Filling one wall of a Hollywood building is an 80-foot likeness of Michael Jackson by Kent Twitchell. Dressed in a white suit, gangster hat, and spats, the singer appears to be dancing across the wall of the old El Capitan Theater. Another Hollywood mural, Tom Suriya's *You Are the Star*, shows dozens of famous entertainers and movie creations, including Marilyn Monroe, John Wayne, R2-D2, and King Kong. As you look at the mural, you realize that these stars, seated in a darkened movie theater, are looking at *you!* True to the title, you are now the star, idolized by the very people you've worshiped on the screen.

Above: Tom Suriya, *You Are the Star,* Wilcox Avenue and Hollywood Boulevard, Los Angeles, 1983. *Right:* David S. Gordon, *Unbridled,* 4th Street and Ocean Park Boulevard, Santa Monica, CA, 1986.

For pure fun, the winner must be David S. Gordon's *Unbridled* in Santa Monica, California. Stretching along a wall for almost a block, the mural shows an apparent escape of merry-go-round horses from the nearby Santa Monica Pier Carousel. The painted horses appear to have broken loose and are jumping off the pier onto the sandy beach. As they gallop away, down the wall, they are transformed into real horses. You can follow the line of once-captive horses as they splash through the surf to freedom. Even in this playful mural, you can discover a message. What do you suppose it is?

HISTORICAL MURALS IN THE UNITED STATES

Throughout the centuries, many cultures—from the ancient Aztecs to the Romans to modern Americans—have celebrated their history and heritage in spectacular mural paintings. Murals are one way to ensure that the people and events that formed a country will be remembered in the future.

Some of the most important commemorative murals in the United States were created during the Great Depression, in the early 1930s. It was a time when people didn't have much money. They were hungry. Jobs were scarce. To help, the government organized several work programs, referred to as the New Deal. People were put to work building and repairing roads, dams, and parks.

One New Deal project assigned out-of-work artists to paint murals on bare walls in public buildings, mainly post offices. The government hoped to boost Americans' low spirits by giving them something to do and by reminding them of their adventurous past. The murals were supposed to say, "Our forefathers and mothers endured hard times, and we can do it now!"

In 1938 in the Granville, Ohio, post office, little-known artist Wendell Jones painted *First Pulpit in Granville.*

Constantino Brumidi, *The Four Seasons*, U.S. Capitol, Washington, D.C., 1855–56.

23

The graceful, emotion-filled mural shows the arrival of the town's founding fathers and mothers at the future site of Granville. The group has just cut down a stately walnut tree (cleverly painted to hide ugly ventilator openings in the wall) to serve as a pulpit for this first meeting in their new home. They have gathered to sing hymns and give thanks for their safe arrival after surviving so many hardships during the long trip over the mountains of western Pennsylvania. The faces of the people reveal a mixture of fear and hope, determination and uncertainty.

Though Wendell Jones was not widely known, Thomas Hart Benton was famous, perhaps America's foremost muralist. His murals show the rough, rowdy, often crude aspects of America's past, such as the cowboy poker players who dominate *Arts of the West*. Benton's paintings were often controversial. Some viewers would have preferred that he gloss over the massacres, lynchings, dishonesty, and greed that cloud American history. But Benton insisted on showing the blemishes of the past, and, as a result, he created murals of tremendous vitality and realism.

One of Benton's best works is at the Museum of the Harry S. Truman Library in Independence, Missouri. *Independence and the Opening of the West*, which Benton worked on from 1959 to 1962, shows a classic frontier scene. Painted around a doorway inside the museum, the mural shows a group of settlers on one side of the doorway preparing to head west on the Oregon Trail. Above the doorway, four settlers with guns confront two Indians. One of the Indians holds his bow threateningly, while the other extends a peace pipe. Benton's mural reminds us of an uncomfortable fact: westward expansion happened at the expense of native people already established on the land. In 1971 a detail of this mural was duplicated on a U.S. postage stamp, commemorating the 150th year of Missouri's statehood.

Constantino Brumidi's paintings in the United States Capitol in Washington, D.C., rank among the most monumental murals in the United States. His frieze (a long, narrow, decorative band, usually painted along the top of a wall) on the interior of the Capitol Rotunda is 300 feet long and 8 feet tall. Brumidi drew all the rotunda designs in 1877, then started working. Unfortunately, he died in 1880, with barely one-third of the frieze completed. Another artist, Filippo Costaggini, was called in to finish the work from Brumidi's designs. But when all the paintings were done, a 13-foot blank space still remained. Brumidi's mural was not completed until 1953 by Allyn Cox.

Thomas Hart Benton, *Independence and the Opening of the West* (detail), Museum of the Harry S. Truman Library, Independence, Missouri, 1959–62.

Thomas Hart Benton:
American Muralist

The artistic life of Thomas Hart Benton was stormy almost from the beginning. The first controversy resulted from his decision to charcoal a picture of a steam locomotive on a newly wallpapered wall of his home when he was eight years old. Although his mother admired the boy's ability, she scolded him soundly. This was the first of many attacks on his work the artist would endure throughout his life.

Always strong-willed, Tom resisted his father's attempts to make a politician of him. After studying in Chicago and Paris, Tom returned to the United States in 1912 and settled in New York. There, over the next 20 years, he began to make a name for himself as a painter of folksy rural scenes. Always in the back of his mind were the scenes and people he'd known as a boy in Neosho, Missouri, where he was born in 1889. From 1923 to 1924, he exhibited in New York a colorful mural based on his childhood observations. It was not well received. Critics called it "too agitated in form and color"—which was precisely the impression Tom had wanted the painting to make.

After the death of his father, Tom returned more and more to his Midwestern roots for inspiration and subject matter. He backpacked through the Ozarks in 1926–27, then turned west. He made his way across the country, observing, drawing, and painting as he went.

Benton's first public mural was completed at the New School for Social Research in New York in 1931. A sprawling, hard-hitting look at city life in America, the mural was full of images some people found offensive: dance halls, political corruption, bars, street-corner lovers, and boxing matches. Art critics hated the painting, but the public flocked to see it.

Probably the biggest controversy in Benton's career surrounded the mural he did for the Missouri State Capitol in Jefferson City in 1935–36. Benton declared that he painted only what he knew to be the truth, about people and his home state. The mural depicted farms and cities, as well as scenes from Mark Twain's *Huckleberry Finn*. But Benton also depicted corrupt political boss Tom Pendergast, Jesse James robbing a bank, and a

America's most famous muralist, Thomas Hart Benton, at work on *Independence and the Opening of the West* in his home state of Missouri

bare-bottomed baby being diapered by his mother. People across the state were outraged by the show of nakedness.

Benton, however, was merely amused. He'd chosen real images that reflected Missouri, the good and the bad. "Art should be a living thing which has meaning for the public in general," he said. He left it at that, except to add later, "If I have any right to make judgments, I would say that the Missouri mural was my best work."

Finally, after several years, "the public in general" did get used to Tom's straightforward style and began to understand his "meaning." His Missouri mural became one of the most popular attractions in the state, and his paintings were soon in great demand. Thomas Hart Benton became one of America's most famous muralists. Although many of his paintings remained controversial, he was invited to decorate walls all over the country. In 1962 his hometown of Neosho, Missouri, held a celebration in his honor, and Benton was escorted to the proceedings by President Harry S. Truman, himself a Missouri native and admirer of Tom's work.

Constantino Brumidi, detail of frieze depicting the Battle of Lexington, U.S. Capitol Rotunda, Washington, D.C., c. 1880.

From the Capitol Rotunda floor 58 feet below the mural, visitors can easily make out the scenes of significant events in American history, including the landing of Columbus in 1492, the arrival of the Pilgrims in 1620, the Battle of Lexington, the reading of the Declaration of Independence, the birth of aviation, and others.

Brumidi painted other murals in the Capitol as well. In the room where the Agriculture Committee met in 1855 (now the House Appropriations Committee room), murals such as *Harvesting Grain with a McCormick Reaper* remind viewers of the key role farmers played in the growth of America. Brumidi's frescoed ceiling of *The Four Seasons* (see page 22) is delightful, with delicate flowers and baby angels.

Focusing on the contributions of various ethnic groups to the heritage of California is *The Great Wall of Los Angeles*. The wall may well be the longest mural in the world. The project, begun in 1976 under the direction of muralist Judith Baca, is a colossal series of 13-foot-high murals that stretches for nearly a mile along a flood-control channel in the San Fernando Valley. Each mural represents a segment in the history of the area. The first shows animals that roamed the area more than 20,000 years ago. Other segments depict the lives of Native Americans, the coming of the Spanish, the World Wars, and the birth of movies. The sweeping cavalcade of images is meant to show how a number of cultures blended to form present-day Los Angeles.

JEWISH ARTS & SCIENCE

Judith Baca, two sections of *The Great Wall of Los Angeles,* Tujunga Wash, Studio City, CA, 1976-present.

Judith Baca:
A Vision of the Future without Fear

"If you don't like the way things are, how can you change them?" That question, which once hung prominently on a bulletin board in Judith Baca's studio in California, could easily be the motto for her life.

Born in Los Angeles, Baca has spent her life working in the city's neighborhoods to bring people of all races and backgrounds together. She does this by painting community murals.

In 1970, Judith, just out of college, landed a job with the L.A. Cultural Affairs Division. Assigned to troubled East Los Angeles, she managed to get rival gang members to stop fighting and join "mural brigades." Under her direction, these former enemies began working together to decorate their neighborhoods with works of art. Because of her success, Baca was named director of the Citywide Mural Project. Over a three-year period, she organized 40 artists and more than 400 young people to create murals throughout the city.

In 1976 the Army Corps of Engineers asked her to do a mural to brighten up Tujunga Wash, a concrete drainage channel in Studio City that was dry most of the year. Judith saw the possibilities immediately and decided to create a full-scale history of the city. Her plan was to focus mainly on the contributions of the city's ethnic minorities, who, she felt, had not been adequately represented in other kinds of histories.

Judith mobilized historians, educators, artists, and hundreds of local people to work on *The Great Wall*, which was the name she gave to the murals. She was also assisted by the U.S. Army, the city of Los Angeles, and the Social and Public Art Resource Center (SPARC), an organization Baca cofounded with Christina Schlesinger and Donna Deith. Teams of young people directed by Judith and other adult artists have painted the murals in the summers, when the channel is dry. At over 2,435 feet, the mural is already the longest in the world.

"I know two things," Judith said about her young partners. "Working on *The Great Wall* definitely improves their mathematics skills. They have to learn how to use a ruler, to add, to multiply, to transfer images from the scale drawings onto the wall. It also gives them a sense of their history."

After the riots in Los Angeles in 1992, SPARC launched a new project called Cultural Explainers. Its purpose is to bring people of various cultures and races together to discuss the things that make people different and the many things that make us all alike. At public meetings, people from the communities hardest hit by the 1992 riots (African American, Korean American, and Latino) talk to each other about their heritage and culture, as well as about their concerns and hopes for the future.

Currently, Judith Baca, along with artists from seven other countries, is at work on *World Wall: A Vision of the Future without Fear,* dedicated to ending war and bringing peoples of the world together. The original idea was to have people gather inside a giant circle created by the murals and talk about peace. The mural in progress has been displayed in Sweden, Russia, Mexico, and Washington, D.C., and it is scheduled to travel to South Africa, Canada, and South Korea. In each country, artists will contribute yet another panel showing their view of what a "future of hope and light" will look like.

But Baca believes the most important art created for this project will be the discussion that happens as people come together. "The *World Wall* is not complete until dialogue occurs," she said. "It is not a static piece sitting in a museum so people can say, 'Oh, isn't that beautiful.' Of course, I hope they say that, but I want to create the arena for discussion. I am not a decorator of buildings."

Judith Baca

31

MEXICAN MURALS

ew murals can match the grandeur of the wall paintings of the "Big Three of Mexico": David Alfaro Siqueiros, José Clemente Orozco, and Diego Rivera. Their historical murals in the National Palace and other public buildings are huge expressions of the drama and violence of Mexico's past.

Siqueiros's mural *Cuauhtémoc Against the Myth*, in the Centro de Artes Realistic Moderno in Mexico City, seems to flow across and down the curving surface behind a staircase. It's an odd, interesting location for a

José Clemente Orozco, *Hidalgo*, Governor's Palace, Guadalajara, Mexico, 1937.

mural, which at first glance seems to show sculptured Aztec and animal figures. Siqueiros said he wanted people to sense the heroism of the early Mexican people who stood against invaders of their land. As viewers move up or down the staircase, they can see different angles and get different impressions of the huge mural. Some people say they feel as if they are actually climbing inside the painting.

The specific historical reference of the painting, however, is to the Aztec emperor Cuauhtémoc. Cuauhtémoc's uncle, Montezuma II, was emperor when the ruthless Spanish explorer Hernán Cortés arrived in Mexico, in 1519. According to an old Aztec story, a powerful god called Quetzalcóatl would one day return to reclaim his kingdom. Quetzalcóatl was described as bearded and pale skinned. When Cortés arrived, fitting the description, Montezuma felt sure this must be Quetzalcóatl. Montezuma opened the royal city to Cortés and his soldiers and presented the Spaniards with gifts.

It quickly became clear, however, that these beings were not gods, and their intentions were far from honorable. But by the time the Aztecs could mount a defense, the slaughter had begun. The Spaniards captured Montezuma and took over the royal city (now Mexico City).

As next in line to the throne, the nephew of Montezuma, Cuauhtémoc, made a valiant attempt to rally his subjects. For a while, he and a small number of Aztecs fought off the invaders. But in the end, the Spanish overwhelmed them. Cuauhtémoc was captured as he tried to escape, and he was later executed by Cortés, ending the Aztec empire. To this day, however, Cuauhtémoc remains a heroic figure in Mexican history.

In Siqueiros's mural, Cuauhtémoc appears to withstand gigantic horse hooves and an uplifted cross with a dagger tip. The symbolism suggests the godlike reverence early Mexicans had for horses, which the people had never seen until the Spanish invaders brought them to Mexico.

The dagger-tipped cross also stands for the Roman Catholic religion; after all, the Spaniards butchered countless people in the name of Christianity. In many ways, the mural is violent and scary, capturing the terror, tragedy, and heroism of Mexican history.

José Clemente Orozco also presents aspects of Mexico's past in his 1948 painting *National Allegory,* which is on the side of the National School for Teachers in Mexico City. In the center of the mural are a hooked eagle's beak and claw separated by the curved shape of a snake. Both represent what Orozco called "the Mexican earth." Blackened ruins on the lower right side of the mural, along with the jutting blade left of center, suggest Mexico's violent past. The gigantic leg of a man climbing on the left, the huge hand placing a block on the right, and the real doorway at bottom center may symbolize Mexico's hope of growth and prosperity.

Many critics consider Diego Rivera the greatest mural painter of all time. His historical paintings sweep across the walls of public buildings throughout Mexico, as well as in the United States. Rivera's murals in the National Palace in Mexico City and the Detroit Institute of Arts are remarkable creations, full of movement and color and hundreds of characters. Although a mere glance at one of these immense murals is enough to spark a reaction, to see every detail and to fully grasp the mural's intricate meaning, you must study it carefully.

Rivera painted a 13-by-50-foot fresco called *Dream of a Sunday Afternoon in*

David Alfaro Siqueiros, *Cuauhtémoc Against the Myth,* Tecpan, Tlatelolco, Mexico, 1944.

Diego Rivera, *Dream of a Sunday Afternoon in the Alameda*, Hotel del Prado, Mexico City, 1948.

the Alameda for the Hotel del Prado in Mexico City in 1948. The painting shows Alameda Park, a large central commons in Mexico City. Rivera imagines all the important people and events that occurred in and around the Alameda over the years. The images reflect the grand panorama of Mexican history.

Among the multitude of figures in the painting are many of the most notorious figures from Mexico's past.

There's Hernán Cortés on the far left, his uplifted bloody hand symbolizing the violence Spanish conquerors inflicted on the native people. Above him in the trees, victims of the Spanish Holy Inquisition wear cone-shaped *coroza,* or dunce caps, which indicated that they were in disgrace.

Just below and to the right, General Santa Anna is shown giving away the keys to Texas, which originally belonged to Mexico.

Throughout the picture, Rivera's friends are intermingled with historical,

artistic, literary, and popular figures. In the lower left corner, for example, a skinny boy is about to pick the pocket of a well-to-do man with his back turned. Rivera said the boy represented the large number of poor street children in Mexico who must make their own way in the streets by begging or stealing.

Diego included himself in the mural, as a little boy standing just left of center and wearing a straw hat and yellow striped socks. His adult wife, the painter Frida Kahlo, stands behind him.

Rivera is holding hands with an over-dressed skeleton, which seems ominous. But the man in the black suit and hat to the right of the skeleton is José Guadalupe Posada. He was a popular Mexican artist who guided Rivera as a young man and whom Diego idolized. The skeleton was a familiar figure in many of Posada's illustrations.

Rivera, Orozco, and Siqueiros were aware that their mural paintings drew on an important tradition. Mayan and Toltec painters had been accomplished muralists as far back as A.D. 800.

Diego Rivera:
Revolutionary with a Paintbrush

"The earliest memory I have," Diego Rivera once wrote, "was that I was drawing." Almost before Diego could walk and talk, he was scribbling pictures on everything he could reach. Finally, in self-defense, his parents set aside a spare room for little Diego's "murals." Later, they arranged blackboards on the walls, which Diego filled with drawings of trains, animals, toys, and soldiers.

Diego María Concepción Juan Nepomuceno Estanislao de la Rivera y Barrientos Acosta y Rodríguez was born in Guanajuato, Mexico, in 1886. His father, a mining chemist and editor of a small liberal newspaper, taught him early to stand up for his beliefs and to fight for his rights.

At the age of 13, Diego was enrolled in the San Carlos Academy of Fine Arts in Mexico City. While in school, he met and developed a friendship with José Guadalupe Posada, the great Mexican folk artist. Posada taught Diego to be aware of the struggles of the common people and influenced his early life and art.

After spending several years in Europe, Diego returned to Mexico to find that conditions had grown miserable and dangerous. Porfirio Díaz, whom Diego had always disliked, had taken over as president. People were afraid to speak out against the dictator, for fear of being killed. Diego offered his support to the rebel movement that was forming. He painted posters advertising the cause and even smuggled ammunition in his paint boxes when he traveled.

As bad as things were, Diego knew he still had much to learn. In 1911 he reluctantly left his native land and returned to France. There he met the great Spanish artist Pablo Picasso and other artists who were painting in the modern style of cubism. Rivera became a success in Europe, working in the cubist style, but he began to realize that he wanted to paint realistic scenes that served a purpose—that helped people in some way.

Then Diego met a fellow Mexican painter, David Siqueiros, who visited

Diego Rivera

Paris in 1919. Rivera and Siqueiros discussed their homeland, agreeing that Mexico needed artists who could inspire people and give them hope in their struggle against dictatorship. Diego decided to eventually go home and paint in the great Mexican mural tradition.

After studying the great European murals for a year and a half, Diego headed back to Mexico, where he began to create murals at an incredible pace. His paintings appeared on walls everywhere, from the University of Mexico to the Ministry of Education. Diego had never felt so alive, and his paintings reflected his feeling. They depicted the harshness of Mexican life, but they showed the joy, too. His murals attacked injustice but praised what was right and fair. Diego believed that people should join together to solve their problems.

Not everyone loved or understood Diego Rivera's art, however. His political views often got him into trouble. Sometimes people misread his intentions, since many of his paintings supported socialism, an unpopular philosophy in the United States.

The biggest controversy of Diego's career happened in 1933, when he was commissioned to paint a mural called *Man at the Crossroads* in the lobby of the new RCA Building at Rockefeller Center in New York City. Rivera included in the painting a portrait of Vladimir Lenin, one of the founders of Russian Communism.

Many people—including the Rockefellers, who owned the building—thought the images were "un-American" and dangerous. The Rockefellers ordered the finished fresco covered so no one could see it. A year later, it was smashed to pieces, and a different painting by another artist was put in its place. Diego was outraged. In 1934, working from his original sketches, he reconstructed the mural in the Palace of Fine Arts in Mexico City, where it still resides.

Aztec artists had decorated the walls of public buildings with elaborate murals. Art historians generally agree that fresco painting originated in Mexico.

Many beautiful murals have been discovered in the earliest known cities of Mesoamerica, the name historians give to the land now known as Mexico and Central America. Places such as Teotihuacán and Bonampak (which means "city of painted walls" in the Mayan language) appear to have been centers for artists to practice their skills.

Skilled painters interpreted the complex Mayan spiritual rites that priests practiced in temples. With bold outlines, using bright reds, yellows, and greens, Mayan muralists reveal their ideas about people's position in the universe. Some ancient murals, especially Mayan paintings, show the human sacrifice and torture that were part of Mesoamerican religious rituals.

Though some of the murals may seem brutal to the modern viewer, they are rich treasure troves of information about those long-gone cultures. One fresco in a room at Bonampak, for example, shows a ceremonial procession of figures in masks accompanied by trumpeters. Several people wear reptile

Mayan fresco from Bonampak depicting dignitaries attending a ritual sacrifice, c. A.D. 600–950, National Museum of Anthropology, Mexico City, Mexico.

masks. One is a crocodile. Another marcher is costumed as a crab, complete with huge pincer gloves. At the bottom, an unmasked man appears to give directions to the others.

The ancient city of Teotihuacán had been destroyed—probably in a war—at least 600 years before the Spanish arrived and conquered the Aztecs. The shining city had flourished for a thousand years, then died. Who its people were and what their lives were like will no doubt remain a mystery. But the murals at Teotihuacán hint at the rich culture that thrived in Mexico long ago. The meanings of many of the symbols and images have been lost. Their beauty remains, however. In the Palace of Quetzalpapalotl, for instance,

jaguars in ceremonial feathered helmets blow giant seashell trumpets. Above them, symbols, possibly with religious significance, form a continuous frieze around the room.

Few countries have a mural tradition as long or enduring as Mexico's. Diego Rivera, the greatest Mexican painter of the 20th century, spoke often of the spirit that moved his ancestors—and him—to create murals. He said, "Above all it had been emotion-centered. It was molded by their hopes, fears, joys, superstitions, and sufferings.

"This tradition was in me, too, buried in my subconscious. Yet I was continually aware of the greatness of pre-Conquest art."

ITALIAN
RENAISSANCE
MURALS

Between the 14th and 16th centuries, artists in Europe enjoyed a time of freedom and an outpouring of public admiration, just as artists had in ancient Mexico. During this period, called the Renaissance, some of the greatest artists of all time painted wall and ceiling murals.

One of the most famous murals in the world is Leonardo da Vinci's *The Last Supper* at the Santa Maria delle Grazie convent in Milan, Italy. The subject of the 14-by-30-foot mural is Christ's final meeting with his disciples before his crucifixion, when he reveals to them that "one of you shall betray me." The apostles react with varying emotions. Some are puzzled.

Opposite page: Paolo Veronese, presumed self-portrait as a hunter, fresco in the Villa Barbaro, Maser, Italy, c. 1560. *Above:* Leonardo da Vinci, *The Last Supper,* Santa Maria delle Grazie, Milan, Italy, 1495–97/8.

Endangered Masterpiece:
The Attempt to Rescue Leonardo's *The Last Supper*

The Last Supper as Leonardo da Vinci painted it no longer exists. The beautiful mural that Leonardo painted in 1497 in the damp basement dining room of a convent has long since turned into powder and crumbled away, leaving only a shadow of its former glory on the wall.

One reason for the destruction is that Leonardo's mural isn't a true fresco; that is, it wasn't painted *into* the wall. It only lies on the surface. It's not that Leonardo was careless. Many Renaissance murals were painted this way. With fresco, an artist has to work very quickly to apply the paint to the wet plaster before the plaster dries. Leonardo apparently wanted more time to work his paint, so he painted on the dry wall.

Another problem is that a natural spring beneath the floor (which Leonardo did not know was there) causes the room to have an extremely high humidity level. All that water in the air has washed away many of the mural's original colors. Experts guess that only about 20 percent of Leonardo's original mural is still present.

To make matters worse, *The Last Supper* was painted over many times through the centuries by less skillful artists in an attempt to save it. Yet, despite the devastation of time, water, and people's misguided efforts to restore the painting, it is once again becoming possible—at least, in part—to see the hand of Leonardo in *The Last Supper*.

Over the last 16 years, in a last-ditch effort to save what is left of the painting, restorers have begun using space-age technology (and incredible patience) to remove years of grime and undo the damage caused by water and previous restorers. After making infrared and ultraviolet analyses of the old painting, they went to work. Gazing through a microscope,

Restorers are working diligently to save Leonardo's famous work, which he painted on the wall of a damp basement.

art experts cleaned away grime and removed paint that, according to chemical tests, had been applied by someone other than Leonardo. At the same time, they reattached tiny pieces of the original that had peeled away. The job was so delicate and tedious that it took a month to clean one square inch of the painting.

After only a few years of work, the results were encouraging. Every day, a *Last Supper* emerged that no one had ever seen before. Details, expressions, and colors that had been hidden came to light. Now, as the restoration nears completion, Leonardo's remarkable skill has become evident, even though much of the original painting is gone. Giuseppina Brambilla, who headed the restoration, said excitedly at one point, "Each day we are discovering a painting of extraordinary beauty. It is like seeing Leonardo for the first time."

Although the restoration has been successful and the masterpiece is saved for future generations, Brambilla isn't sure the master himself would like the results. "I do think that Leonardo would be very disappointed if he saw his painting today because it isn't the same painting that he created. He would find himself before a work that has been trampled by the passage of time and by the passage of man."

Others are angry, sad, or doubtful. The bearded Judas frowns. He leans away from Jesus, unluckily spilling the salt as he does so.

Many people consider Michelangelo's ceiling fresco in the Sistine Chapel in Rome the greatest accomplishment in the history of art. The artist worked for four years lying on his back atop a scaffold 60 feet above the ground. Spread across nearly 6,000 square feet, the fresco is divided into many geometrical sections. They interpret the biblical stories of the Creation, the Fall of Man, and the Atonement.

Unfortunately, it is difficult to fully appreciate the ceiling mural unless you

Above: Detail of the Sistine Chapel ceiling. *Opposite page:* Michelangelo, ceiling, Sistine Chapel, Vatican Palace, Vatican State. (Note: the detail above is from a different section of the ceiling than the one shown opposite.)

are lying on your back. To see the mural from the floor of the chapel, a viewer must lean backward in an uncomfortable position. (The view is worth it, though!)

While Michelangelo was busy painting the ceiling of the Sistine Chapel, other artists were decorating other parts of the Vatican. One of these was Raphael, who painted two 18-foot arched murals, *Dispute of the Sacrament* and *The School of Athens,* on facing walls in the papal apartments.

Dispute of the Sacrament (known in Italian as the *Disputa)* shows church officials, prophets, saints, and Christ himself involved in what appears to be a heated religious debate. At the time the mural was painted, debates about all sorts of spiritual matters were common. People argued about the size and shape of heaven, what angels looked like, and the true number of saints. In this painting, the leaders of the church are more likely agreeing, not arguing, on the meaning of the Eucharist (communion) going on in the center.

What makes the *Disputa* unique is Raphael's subtle, varied shades of color and his formal, pyramid-shaped composition. If you look closely, you can see the internal form of the painting— gently sweeping arcs and a perfect pyramid. The earthly figures at the bottom form one arc, while the saints in heaven form another, upward arc. The radiating lines at the top and center of the painting, which give it a sort of halo, are made of raised stucco. The

Above: Raphael, *The Dispute of the Sacrament,* Stanza della Segnatura, Vatican Palace, Vatican State, 1510–11. *Right:* A diagram reveals the composition of the painting, formed of arcs and a pyramid.

lines help direct the viewer's eye to the top of the pyramid, where God stands above Christ on his throne.

These invisible lines show the compositional plan that Raphael used. It's one that many artists have since admired and imitated.

The composition of the painting gives the sense of a perfectly ordered universe. The pointing figure to the right of the altar directs the viewer's eye upward to heaven. The geometrical structure of the *Disputa* makes clear what people living during the Renaissance believed about the relationship between heavenly beings and humans: human thoughts and ambitions should turn up toward God, the center of the universe.

The School of Athens is one of Raphael's most vibrant frescoes. Showing a number of great philosophers engaged in vigorous discussion, the mural is less formal than *Dispute.* We seem to

Raphael, *The School of Athens,* Stanza della Segnatura, Vatican Palace, Vatican State, 1510–11.

Benozzo Gozzoli, *The Adoration of the Magi*, Palazzo Medici-Riccardi, Florence, Italy, 1459.

be looking down a long hallway, beautifully arched so the eye is drawn farther and farther back to the blue sky and clouds outside. In the center, two important philosophers of ancient Greece, Aristotle and Plato, appear to be walking toward us. Around them, Pythagorus (the bearded reader, left), Socrates (sprawled on the steps, middle), Euclid (drawing with a compass, lower right), and dozens of other great thinkers sit or stand in informal groups, engaged in discussion. Raphael painted Plato (at center, in red robe, pointing upward) as a portrait of the elderly Leonardo da Vinci, probably as a tribute to the artist, whom he admired. And Raphael included himself in this masterpiece, too. That's him, with the long neck, peering outward from the group at the lower right.

Raphael uses light almost magically in *The Liberation of St. Peter*, a fresco in another room of the Vatican. The mural is based on a story from the book of Acts in the New Testament. After being thrown into prison by the Roman king Herod, the disciple Peter is rescued by one of God's angels. On the left in the painting, stunned soldiers gesture in disbelief as the angel bends to awaken Peter. On the right, the scene flows into an image of the dazed saint being led to safety past unconscious guards. The light in the details is extraordinary: the pale moon in the upper left, the first glimmer of dawn on the hillside below, the glow of the soldier's torch on the steps, and the radiance of the angel, which sets the entire painting ablaze.

Benozzo Gozzoli's *The Adoration of the Magi* represents the three kings on their journey to visit the newborn Jesus in Bethlehem. The painting also serves as a portrait of members of the powerful Medici family, who are pictured prominently in the lower foreground, along with their household staff, influential friends, and business partners. Gozzoli himself stands in the crowd, wearing a cap bearing his signature, *Opus Benotii*. (In Latin, this means "Work by Benozzo.")

The Medicis were one of the most powerful and notorious families in history. Cosimo, who lived from 1389 to 1464, was called the "father of his country" for his achievement in making Florence, Italy, the center of power and culture during the early Renaissance. Like his grandfather, Lorenzo de Medici (1449–1492) charmed the people of Florence, even though he exercised almost absolute power by the age of 25. Lorenzo the Magnificent, as he was called, was a patron of the arts, and under him the Italian Renaissance flourished. The Medici power grew when two family members were elected pope. The family's influence reached its peak in 1533, when Catherine de Medici married Henry II of France.

This was the family for whom Gozzoli painted *The Adoration of the Magi*. He knew how to please these rulers— today his painting would probably be considered good public relations. When guests came to call on the Medicis and worshiped with the family in their private chapel, they might see themselves in a painting on the wall. They would likely feel flattered and honored, which is exactly how merchants want their business associates to feel.

Not all the masterpieces of the Renaissance dealt with religious subjects, though. An assistant to Raphael, Giulio Romano, painted an amazing trompe l'oeil fresco that occupies one whole wall in the Palazzo del Tè in Mantua, Italy. *(Trompe l'oeil* paintings are meant to "trick the eye" by creating an illusion of reality.) *The Fall of the Giants*, painted from 1532–34, was intended to make spectators feel as though they'd been caught in the middle of a catastrophic earthquake. Legend has it that when the flames in a fireplace in the room illuminated the

Giulio Romano, *The Fall of the Giants*, Palazzo del Tè, Mantua, Italy, 1532–34.

Paolo Veronese, Giustiniana Barbaro and the wet nurse with dog, fresco in the Villa Barbaro, Maser, Italy, c. 1560.

painting, it appeared to come to life. Some viewers reportedly had to turn away from the dizzying spectacle to maintain their balance.

In the cross-shaped salon of the Villa Barbaro in Maser, Italy, Paolo Veronese's trompe l'oeil mural amazes and delights. Almost everything in the room, including columns, statues, arches, a satyr's mask, the door, even the little girl peeking out, is a painted illusion. A visitor almost has to walk up and touch the fresco to be sure it's only a flat wall. A lady, her servant, and a dog look out from a balcony overhead. Children, animals, and a dignified man in a hunting outfit (see page 42)—which may be a portrait of Veronese himself—appear in false openings and peep around painted walls. Visitors feel like they are in a busy, crowded villa, but it's all an illusion.

EARLY CHRISTIAN MURALS

Jesus Christ was born into a world that was largely Roman. The vast Roman Empire spread out in all directions—from North Africa to Asia Minor to Britain. By 21 B.C., the only lands Rome did not control were either too far away to reach or were still unknown. When Caesar Augustus died in A.D. 14, Rome was a glorious city of palaces and public theaters. During this Golden Age of Rome, Roman citizens valued learning, honor, and duty to the Olympian gods.

The empire Augustus established

Romanesque, *Christ Pantocrator,* Church of San Clemente, Tahull, c. 1125. Museum of Catalan Art, Barcelona, Spain.

lasted nearly 500 years, until A.D. 476. Over the centuries, by means of a strict legal system and a powerful army, Roman rulers tried to control their far-flung subjects. Because the empire engulfed so many different nationalities, races, religions, and cultures, it became increasingly difficult for one emperor and one army to keep them all under control. Rebellions broke out and the Roman army struggled to maintain power.

Almost immediately after the death of Jesus, his followers began to preach his gospel. Christianity quickly spread during the first century A.D. from Judea, where Jesus was born, to Antioch, to Corinth, and on to Rome.

55

During the early centuries after the death of Jesus, Christianity was seen as a threat to the "divinity" of the Roman emperors. Converts to Christianity were persecuted. In Rome, to practice their religion in safety, Christians went underground into the cavelike catacombs, or tombs, of the city. Here, among the bones of kings and common people, early Christians gathered to worship in secret. If they were caught at prayer, they could be executed for their beliefs. Perhaps to lighten the gloomy atmosphere, early Christians painted the walls and ceilings in some of the dark catacombs.

These early Christian murals can still be seen in the ancient burial chambers in Rome. A sketchy ceiling painting in the Catacomb of Saints Peter and Marcellinus in Rome, for example, shows the brilliance achieved by amateur artists in the spirit of devotion.

Persecution of Christians ended in the fourth century A.D., when the emperor Constantine gave Christians freedom of worship. Then he made a move that would end the Roman Empire and change the world forever. In A.D. 330 Constantine moved the capital of the empire to the Greek city of Byzantium (now Istanbul, Turkey) and changed its

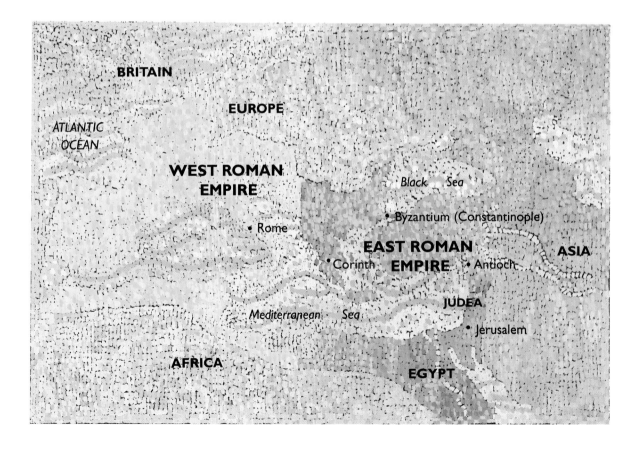

Roman, fresco, Catacomb of Saints Peter and Marcellinus, Rome, Italy, c. 3rd century.

name to Constantinople. For the next 1,000 years, this city would be a cultural center. In the west, Rome fell to fierce barbarians who attacked and pillaged it repeatedly.

The Byzantines carried on many Roman traditions—with a difference. Since the Christian city of Constantinople was in the Middle East, it came under the influence of old Greek traditions. By about A.D. 500, this mixture of cultures had produced a new, distinctive style of art and architecture known as Byzantine. Ornate, colorful, and stately, Byzantine art emphasizes the spiritual significance of earthly things.

Throughout the Byzantine Empire, Christianity spread and art flourished. Holy images—called icons—appeared as mosaics and frescoes on church walls and ceilings throughout Europe and the Near East. Like the artists of Mesoamerica and artists in the Renaissance, the painters of these murals were not interested in mere decoration. They wanted to express the deeply felt emotion of their new faith.

An important Christian mosaic was crafted around A.D. 400 in the Santa Pudenziana, a church in Rome. This mural is one of the first representations of Jesus Christ and possibly established the model of how he would be portrayed for centuries to come: robed and bearded, with flowing dark hair. The play of light across jutting pieces of colored stones gives the huge mosaic a shimmering vibrancy.

In A.D. 527, Justinian I ascended the Byzantine throne. Under him and his

gifted wife, Empress Theodora, some important old Roman traditions were reestablished, especially the legal system. Under Justinian's direction, scholars assembled the Code of Laws, which still stands as the basis for the legal system in many countries. The emperor also supervised the construction of many architectural masterpieces, including the domed church of the Hagia Sophia in Constantinople (Istanbul).

The finest examples of Byzantine mosaics created during Justinian's reign can be found not in Istanbul, however, but in Ravenna, Italy. Two stunning mosaics were created there in the choir area of the Church of San Vitale. *The Court of Justinian* and *The Court of Empress Theodora* date from about A.D. 547. The mosaics' gold, red, and green tiles are inlaid so perfectly that from below they look like rich carpets or woven tapestries.

The mosaics at San Vitale show the haloed emperor Justinian and his wife bringing gifts—a golden bowl and a jeweled cup—to honor Jesus. Empress Theodora's purple robe is embroidered with a scene of the Wise Men bringing gifts to Jesus. These murals illustrate the connection between the earth and the spiritual world, as most Byzantine art does.

Byzantine, *The Court of Empress Theodora,* San Vitale, Ravenna, Italy, c. A.D. 547.

Mural in the Reformed Church of Waltensburg, Switzerland, c. 1350.

Images of Jesus and the saints decorated the walls of churches and cathedrals throughout Europe and the Middle East. Placed high on church walls, the murals taught worshipers, most of whom could not read or write, the principles of their faith. The murals helped people understand the mysterious stories—the miracles, the Resurrection, the Ascension. The size and beauty of the paintings filled worshipers with as much awe as did the stories themselves.

The development of Byzantine art was interrupted in 726 by a century-long debate called the Iconoclastic Controversy. The battle nearly destroyed the Byzantine Empire. The dispute focused on the place and function of icons in churches. Early Christians had inherited from Judaism the idea that worshiping idols was sinful. In the West, worship of holy images of Jesus and the Virgin Mary had become obsessive. Alarmed by these reports, Emperor Leo III ordered all icons removed from churches. He mobilized his army to enforce the iconoclasm. (Iconoclasm means the breaking or destruction of holy images.)

Many clergy, especially monks in Western Europe, were killed as they tried to defend the murals or mosaics in their churches. Bloody riots sometimes broke out in towns when Leo's iconoclasts arrived. By the time the controversy subsided, around 850, nearly every holy image in Europe had been destroyed. When the debate ended, however, Byzantine art entered its second golden age, and more magnificent icons were created.

Religious fervor grew in medieval Europe. By the 11th century, the "Dark Ages" were over and troops of pilgrims and holy wanderers were taking to the roads in search of salvation, healing, and other "blessings of the saints." On foot or on horseback, these "palmers," as they sometimes called themselves, often trekked hundreds of miles to holy shrines. Among the most popular destinations were Rome and Monte Gargano in Italy, Canterbury Cathedral in England, the Shrine of St. Compostella in Spain, and Jerusalem. There were few inns or taverns along the road, so the palmers frequently sought refuge in churches and monasteries. When they knelt to pray, they often looked up into the faces of Jesus and the Virgin Mary painted on walls and ceilings.

One such place is the Church of San Clemente in the village of Tahull in western Catalonia, Spain. An inspiring fresco, *Christ Pantocrator*, looms in the semishadows of the curved ceiling overhead (see page 54). Surrounded by the apostles, the gigantic figure of Jesus sits enthroned, one hand raised and the other clutching a book inscribed with the Latin motto, "I am the light of the world."

MURALS OF ANCIENT ROME AND EGYPT

As long ago as 2,000 years before the Christian age, Indian, Egyptian, and Roman artists were at work decorating the walls of homes and tombs, preserving their cultures' religious and historical heritage, and showing off their skills. Regrettably, many of their achievements now lie in ruins. In some cases, only fragments of the original murals remain to give us a glimpse of their former glory. It's clear, however, that mural painting was highly valued in ancient times.

When Mt. Vesuvius erupted without warning in A.D. 79, the nearby cities of Pompeii and Boscoreale vanished beneath an avalanche of ash and lava. It was a tragedy for the thousands of people who died in those Italian cities. But the calamity did give modern historians who uncovered the towns an opportunity to study Roman life preserved almost as it had been on that fateful day so long ago.

Archeologists have discovered wonderful murals and mosaics in villas such as those at Boscoreale. The owners of these luxurious country homes apparently hired artists to create wall paintings that would inspire, comfort, and brighten—the same reasons we decorate our homes today.

Roman, *Toilette of the Bride*, Villa of the Mysteries, Pompeii, Italy, c. 50 B.C.

Roman, Villa of the Mysteries, Pompeii, Italy, c. 50 B.C.

One home unearthed at Boscoreale is decorated with several trompe l'oeil murals. One scene seems to look out onto a perfect villa. Sunlight falls on buildings and a beautifully detailed gate and wall. Ornate columns stand in the foreground, and a painted marble border runs around the whole room. At the top of the mural is a temple, indicating the importance of religion to ancient Romans.

Religious feeling is evident also in what has come to be known as the Villa of the Mysteries in Pompeii. Even though scholars aren't sure exactly what the people in the pictures are doing or who painted them, the murals are impressive. Against a brilliant red background, life-size figures move gracefully on a narrow ledge. Some art historians believe the frieze depicts some kind of religious initiation ceremony—perhaps the rites involved with women's passage into maturity or marriage. And since the god Bacchus (Dionysus) is pictured prominently in the mural, it probably shows rites performed in his worship.

Like the Greeks, whose art the Romans copied, ancient Romans enjoyed decorating their homes with colorful mosaics. Beautiful mosaics, such as those at the House of the Faun, were discovered at Pompeii. One spectacular 9-by-17-foot mosaic floor, created in about 100 B.C., shows the historic Battle of Issus, which occurred in 333 B.C., between Alexander the Great and Persian King Darius III (see page 66). Although the mosaic is damaged and most likely a copy of an earlier Greek painting, its vivid colors and action-packed scenes are still visible.

King Darius, wild-eyed and gesturing, watches from his chariot as the young, determined Macedonian general, Alexander, bears down on him. The charioteer behind Darius whips his black horses furiously. A dead tree sticks up in the background and many spears jut upward while the violence of the battle explodes across the mural.

This mosaic is unusual because the artist used extremely small tiles—up to fifty for every inch of picture. That makes the detail and colors very sharp and precise. For example, note the intensity of the expression on the dying warrior's face, which is mirrored in his shield as it tumbles on top of him. The colors the artist used—red, yellow, black, and white—imitate the style of the earlier Greek work from which the mosaic is copied. The colors also give the impression of a dusty, bloody battlefield.

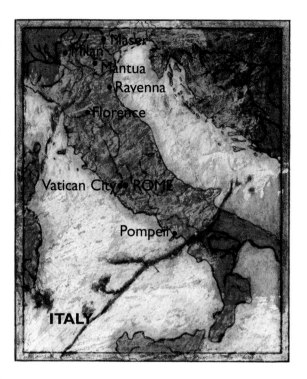

No ancient murals are in better condition than those of the ancient Egyptians. Their magnificent tomb decorations, preserved for many centuries by the dry climate in Egypt, teach us as much about Egyptian culture and religion as about the techniques of their art. The Egyptians believed in eternal life, and the pictures and sacred writings they painted on the walls of the tombs of kings, queens, and nobles were thought to remain with them in the afterlife.

Some lovely Egyptian murals are in the tomb of Queen Nefertari, whose name means "the most beautiful." As wife of the great pharaoh Ramses II, who reigned from about 1290 to 1224 B.C., Nefertari was buried with all the

Above: Roman, *The Battle of Issus,*
mosaic from the House of the Faun, Pompeii,
c. 100 B.C. (Museo Archeologico Nazionale,
Naples, Italy). *Left:* Detail showing Alexander
the Great from *The Battle of Issus.*

splendor due her rank. The superb wall paintings in the queen's tomb depict scenes from her life and visualize her joyously entering the next life. One painting shows Nefertari dressed in a beautiful gown, playing senet, a popular Egyptian board game sort of like checkers.

Another painting, over the entrance to Nefertari's burial chamber, shows her with outstretched wings, like a giant bird. Inside the burial chamber, painted in blazing colors, are pictures of the gods: green-faced Osiris; jackal-headed Anubis, protector of the dead; beetle- and falcon-faced representations of the sun god Re. Most of the deities hold the sacred ankh, symbol of eternal life. All around are hieroglyphic picture writings from the Book of the Dead, which describes Egyptian beliefs about death and immortality.

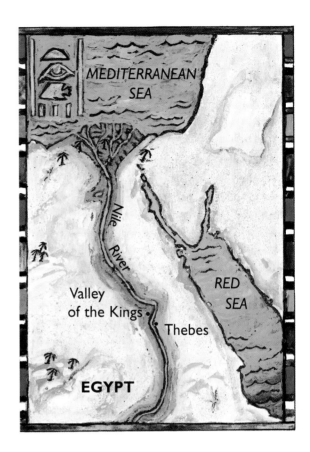

Egyptian, interior of the tomb of Nefertari in the Valley of the Queens, Thebes, Egypt, c. 1300 B.C.

Egyptian Tomb Paintings:
Doorways to the Afterlife

Unlike most murals, Egyptian tomb paintings were never meant to be seen by living eyes. They are extraordinarily beautiful and full of intricate detail. But that's not because the artists hoped people would appreciate them in years to come. The reason had to do with the spiritual purpose of tomb paintings: to ensure a pleasant afterlife.

Egyptian artists, or "scribes," as they were called, made paintbrushes from the stems of rushes (grasslike, hollow-stemmed plants that grow abundantly along rivers and streams), which were chewed at the ends to form stiff bristles. For painting larger areas, artists probably tied together plant stems that had been beaten at the end to separate them into fibers. The result was a thick brush. The paints themselves were natural substances, such as chalk, charcoal, iron oxides, yellow ocher, and copper ore, mixed with plant gums and water.

Most tomb paintings were done in several stages, by a team of people. Working by lamp or torchlight, workers first filled and smoothed the rough stone walls with mud and plaster. After this, the walls were washed with a background color—dull gray, white, or yellow—and a grid of squares was drawn to guide the scribes. Then an artist either chiseled or drew the main outlines of the mural scenes onto the wall. Finally, other scribes filled in the designs with colors and shadings.

The identity or fame of any individual artist was not important. The paintings were not done for the glory of the artist but for the continuation of the life of the person buried in the tomb.

Egyptian, wall painting from the tomb of Nebamun, Thebes, Egypt, c. 1500 B.C. (British Museum, London, England).

Another fascinating mural was found at Thebes in the tomb of Nebamun. According to elaborate lettering on the tomb's walls, Nebamun was "a scribe and counter of grain," which means he was a very important man. One scene shows Nebamun and his family engaging in a favorite Egyptian sport, bird hunting, in the tall reeds along the Nile River. The nobleman in the painting is standing in a thin papyrus boat preparing to hurl a stick in the shape of a snake at a flock of birds. His hunting cat is shown catching a bird by the wing. With Nebamun in the boat is his daughter, who clutches his leg with one

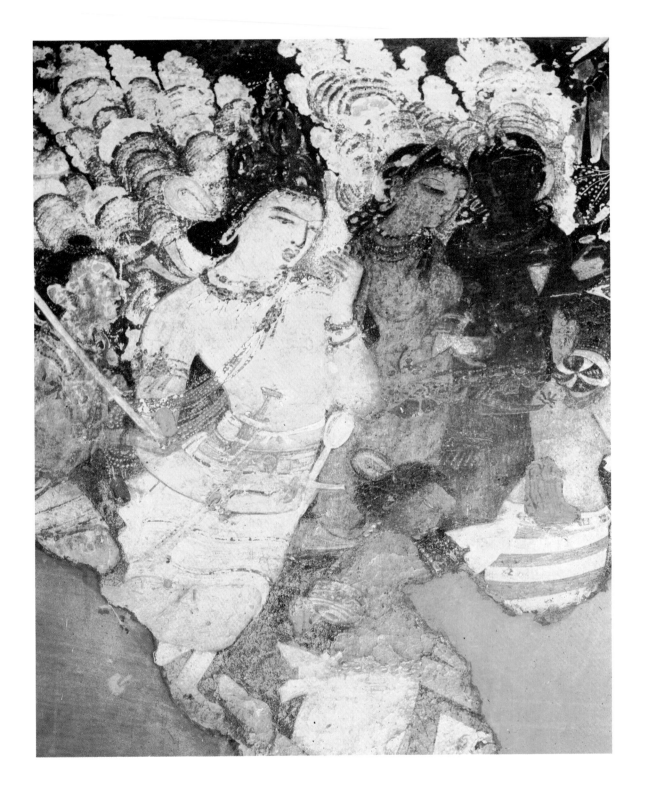

hand and picks a flower with the other. His overdressed wife, looking as though she's on her way to a formal banquet, stands stiffly at the back of the boat. The water below teems with fish, and the air is alive with birds and butterflies.

The purpose of this tomb painting is to ensure that even after death, the nobleman and his family would enjoy pleasant activities together eternally. The hieroglyphic lettering in the mural describes how Nebamun is "seeing what is good in the place of eternity."

At Ajanta, in central India, paintings adorn the walls in a series of adjoining caves cut into a cliff overlooking a river valley. The temple caves and the paintings inside were made from around 200 B.C. through A.D. 200 by generations of Buddhist monks. They came to this remote spot to pray, worship, and find inner peace. People journeyed to Ajanta to seek instruction, advice, and inspiration from the monks—and to see the brilliant paintings.

The murals, many of which are now in ruins, showed scenes from the life of the Buddha. The paintings were apparently meant to be read like a book. As the viewer moved along in a clockwise direction, perhaps performing rituals as he went, he could watch the events unfold in the life of the great prophet. In addition, many murals at Ajanta depict bodhisattva, holy men who, in the Buddhist tradition, gave up their own comfort and safety in order to help others reach salvation, much like Christian saints. What remains of the Ajanta murals reveals a way of life long forgotten.

Indian, cave painting at Ajanta, India, c. 200 B.C. to A.D. 200.

CAVE PAINTINGS

What might be considered the oldest murals ever done were also painted on the walls of caves. They were created many centuries before those at Ajanta—an almost unbelievable 17,000 years ago, in fact. Painted on the walls of the Lascaux cave in southwestern France are hundreds of gigantic bulls, horses, and deer. They were left behind by artists so distant in time we can only guess what they might have been like.

Prehistoric muralists stood on crude scaffolding to reach high up the rough walls. Working by the flickering light of lamps, these early muralists created their art. The evidence of their labor can be seen throughout the cave.

In the chamber of the cave called the Hall of Bulls, four gigantic bulls dominate the smaller figures of horses and other animals. One of these bulls, painted in red, is more than 18 feet long. The room is literally a stampede of animals, and the effect is said to be hypnotic. People who have seen them say they were overwhelmed by the color and sense of motion. (The caves are no longer open to the public.)

Strangest of all, however, is the eight-foot picture of a creature sometimes referred to as "the unicorn," even though it has two horns. With its

Paleolithic, cave painting at Lascaux, France, c. 15,000 B.C.

heavy body, stubby tail, and odd, bearded face, the creature is unlike any known animal. Some historians have suggested that the figure isn't meant to be a real animal. Maybe it was inspired by a dream, or perhaps the creature was painted in the spirit of fun or play.

Archeologists know that people did not *live* in this cave. Hunters came to Lascaux on special occasions for celebrations or religious rituals. They may have painted the cave pictures as a way to "capture" the spirits of the animals they depended on for food.

Whatever the reasons they were done, cave paintings are viewed by art historians as the very beginning of art as we know it. Many people who have visited Lascaux or the Altamira cave in southern Spain, where red, black, and yellow bison, horses, and wild boars gallop across a 45-foot wall, have been amazed at how similar to modern art the cave paintings are.

Over the years, artists such as American painter Elaine de Kooning have been inspired to recapture in their own work the movement and scope of those ancient murals. After a visit to Lascaux and Altamira, de Kooning remarked, "I felt a tremendous identification with those Paleolithic artists. I found myself deep in the caves imagining that I was one of them.... I felt I was coming home." Her *Blue Bison* and *High Wall*, part of a 9-by-20-foot triptych (a painting made up of three panels or sections) shows how much she was affected by those ancient paintings.

When Pablo Picasso visited Lascaux, he is said to have exclaimed, "We have invented nothing!" It's true that the shapes, colors, and patterns of many of his paintings have sometimes been compared to ancient art. Like de Kooning, Picasso no doubt recognized in those cave murals the truth and spirit that artists of every age have struggled to put into their creations. He must have realized the bond between the person who climbed a scaffold to paint the walls of a cave nearly 20,000 years ago and the one who mounts a ladder to decorate a city building today.

Opposite top: Paleolithic, cave painting at Altamira, Spain, c. 15,000 B.C. *Opposite bottom:* Paleolithic, cave painting at Lascaux, France, c. 15,000 B.C.

GLOSSARY

Byzantine art ◆ art of the eastern Roman Empire, associated especially with the reign of Emperor Justinian (A.D. 527–565). Byzantine art deals with the balance of earthly and spiritual concerns. The Byzantine style influenced art in Europe for over 1,000 years.

composition ◆ the arrangement of elements in a work of art; the art of arranging these elements, such as shapes, forms, and colors, in a harmonious or expressive way.

cubism ◆ a movement in modern art initiated in 1907 by Pablo Picasso with his painting *Desmoiselles d'Avignon*. Cubists aimed to break down and take apart the forms of nature and to reconstruct them as geometric elements such as cubes and angles. Another goal of cubism is to show several aspects of a figure or object at the same time.

fresco ◆ painting done on plaster while it is still wet

frieze ◆ a decorative band, usually painted along the top of a wall

icon ◆ an image, painting, or mosaic of a sacred or holy person, associated especially with the eastern Christian church. Icons are also regarded as sacred themselves.

mastic ◆ the cement used in making a mosaic

mosaic ◆ a picture or pattern created by cementing small pieces of stone, glass, or other material to a surface

mural ◆ a painting on a wall, ceiling, or floor

perspective ◆ the portrayal of depth (three dimensions) on a flat (two-dimensional) surface, such as a canvas

Renaissance ◆ a time in Europe, particularly Italy, between the 14th and 17th centuries, marked by a flowering of the arts and a revival or "rebirth" of interest in Greek and Roman traditions

still life ◆ a painting of inanimate (nonliving) objects

tempera ◆ a method of painting in which ground pigments are mixed with egg yolk

tesserae ◆ the small pieces of glass, stone, or other material used in making a mosaic

triptych ◆ a painting in three panels or parts hinged together or hung side by side

trompe l'oeil ◆ a style of painting so realistic that the viewer mistakes the painting (or sculpture) for a real object

FOR FURTHER READING

Adams, Henry. *Thomas Hart Benton: An American Original.* New York: Alfred A. Knopf, 1989.

Art in the United States Capitol. House Doc. No. 94–660. Washington, D.C.: U.S. Gov. Printing Office, 1978.

Barnett, Alan W. *Community Murals: The People's Art.* Philadelphia: The Alliance Press, 1984.

Barthelmeh, Volker. *Street Murals.* New York: Alfred A. Knopf, 1982.

Capek, Michael. *Artistic Trickery: The Tradition of Trompe L'Oeil Art.* Minneapolis: Lerner Publications, 1995.

Drescher, Timothy W. *San Francisco Murals: Community Creates Its Muse.* Pogo Press, 1991.

Gleiter, Jan, and Kathleen Thompson. *Diego Rivera.* Milwaukee: Raintree Publishers, 1989.

Goldstein, Ernest. *Diego Rivera: Journey of Hope.* Minneapolis: Lerner Publications, 1996.

James, T.G.H. *Egyptian Painting and Drawing in the British Museum.* Cambridge, MA: Harvard University Press, 1986.

Levick, Melba, photographer. *The Big Picture: Murals of Los Angeles.* Boston: Little, Brown, & Co., 1988.

Merken, Stefan, and Betty Merken. *Wall Art: Megamurals and Supergraphics.* Philadelphia: Running Press, 1987.

Milman, Miriam. *Trompe L'Oeil Painting: The Illusion of Reality.* New York: Rizzoli, 1982.

Neimark, Anne E. *Diego Rivera: Artist of the People.* New York: Harper-Collins, 1992.

Rigaud, J.P., "Treasures from the Stone Age: Lascaux Cave," *National Geographic* 174, October 1988, 482–499.

Yeo, Wilma, and Helen K. Cook. *Maverick with a Paintbrush.* Garden City, NY: Doubleday and Company, 1977.

INDEX

Kent Twitchell, *Harbor Freeway Overture,* Los Angeles, California.

Acknowledgments

The photographs and illustrations in this book are reproduced courtesy of: pp. 2, 12, 19, 20, 21, 29, 80, © Nancy Hoyt Belcher; p. 6, M. Bryan Ginsberg; p. 8 (left), Tromploy Studio and Gallery, Inc.; pp. 8 (right), 9, Richard Haas; pp. 10, 42, 43, 47, 48, 52, 53, 54, 57, 58–59, 62, 64, 66, Scala/Art Resource, NY; pp. 15, 25, 60, 67, A.A.M. van der Heyden, Narden, The Netherlands; pp. 16–17, © Wyland Studios, Inc.; p. 18, Ringling Bros. and Barnum & Bailey Combined Shows, Inc.; pp. 22, 28, Architect of the Capitol; p. 27, UPI/Bettmann; p. 31, Social and Public Art Resource Center; p. 32, © John Neubauer; p. 35, reproduction with permission from the National Institute of Arts and Literature, Mexico; pp. 36–37, Robert Schalkwijk; pp. 39, 46, 74 (top), The Bettmann Archive; p. 40, SEF/Art Resource, NY; pp. 45, 49, 50, Erich Lessing, Art Resource, NY; p. 69, Werner Forman/Art Resource, NY; p. 70, Borromeo/Art Resource, NY; pp. 72, 74 (bottom), French Government Tourist Office. Diagram on p. 48 and maps on pp. 41, 56, 65, 67 are by John Erste.

FRANKLIN PIERCE COLLEGE LIBRARY

00096417